MY AMAZING PRESCHOOLER
LEARNING SERIES

Let's Learn About BUGS

My First Book About Bugs
for Preschoolers (ages 3–5)

by Lee Zander

TWORAVENS
B O O K S

Two Little Ravens
CHILDREN'S NON-FICTION BOOKS

Paperback Edition: 9781968080006
Hardcover Edition: 9781968080013
Digital Edition: 9781968080020

Published in the United States by Two Ravens Books LLC,
254 Chapman Rd, Ste 209, Newark DE 19702

'Expand the mind, free the imagination, one title at a time.'
www.tworavensbooks.com

Welcome to
"Let's Learn About Bugs"

This delightful book invites young learners to explore the fascinating world of bugs. From ladybugs wearing polka-dot coats to dragonflies zooming like helicopters, each page introduces a new creature, accompanied by fun facts and playful language.

Designed for curious preschoolers, the book is filled with silly surprises that make learning about insects an engaging adventure.

This book supports early learning by building vocabulary and encouraging joyful read-aloud experiences as part of the Let's Learn series. Whether you're a parent, guardian, or educator, you'll find this book to be a valuable tool for sparking curiosity and fostering a love of nature in young children.

Enjoy the adventure!

Lee Zander

Ladybugs wear RED coats with BLACK polka dots!

Beetles wear shiny armor like tiny knights!

Ants march in line like a tiny parade!

Bumblebees bounce from flower to flower, busy as can be.

Butterflies start as crawling caterpillars before they fly.

Caterpillars munch on leaves for breakfast, lunch, and dinner!

Honeybees dance to tell friends where flowers are.

Cicadas sing loud songs in the summer sun.

Crickets play music by rubbing their wings together.

Dragonflies zoom like helicopters over the pond.

Spiders spin sticky webs to catch their dinner.

Grasshoppers hop high and have happy hopping contests.

Fireflies glow at night, having their own light show.

Glow worms light up caves like tiny lanterns.

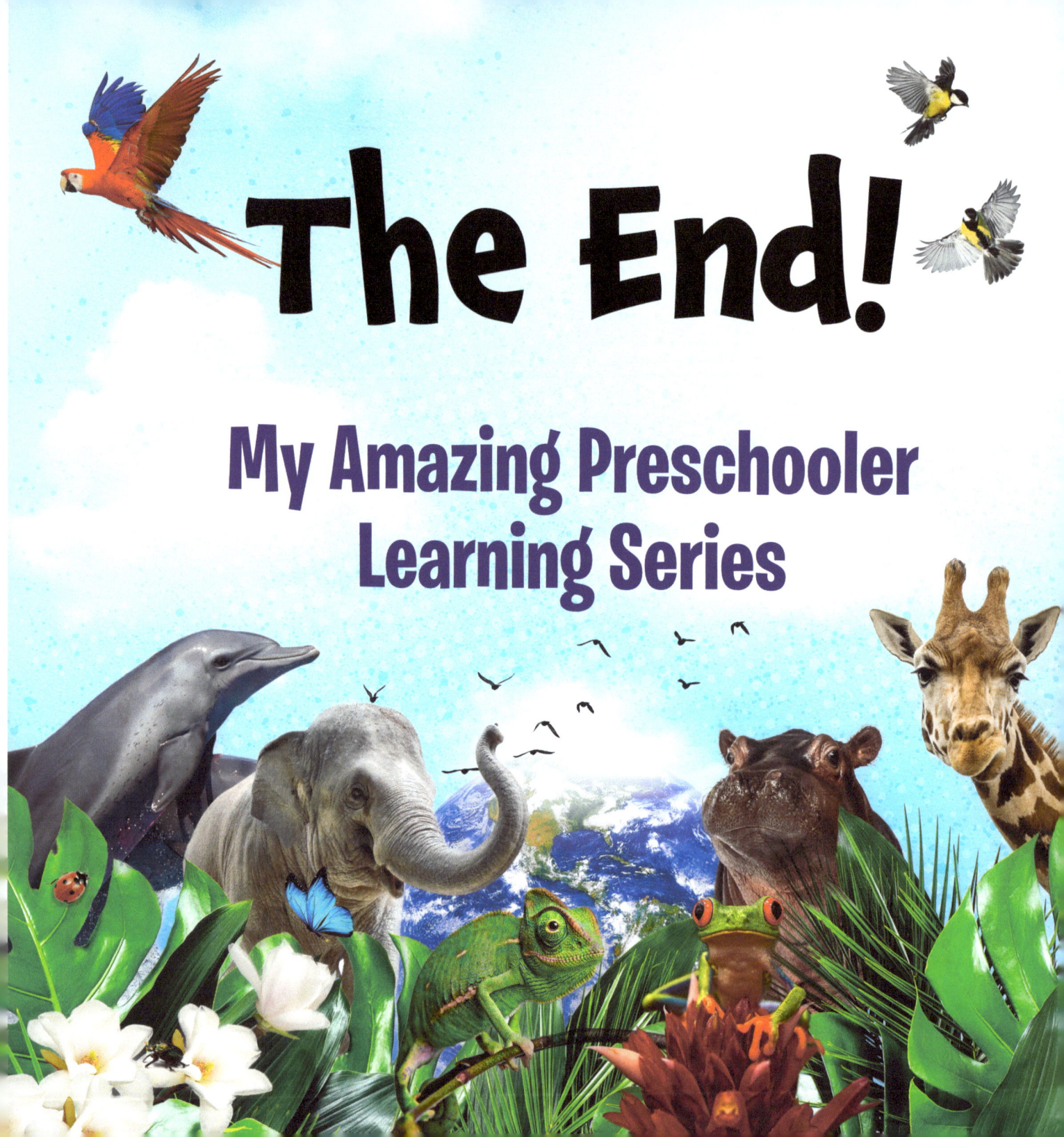

The End!

My Amazing Preschooler Learning Series

Dear Amazing Reader,

Thank you for reading **Let's Learn About Bugs!** I hope it brought joy and sparked curiosity during your read-aloud time together.

If you enjoyed this book, I would be grateful if you would take a minute to let me know by posting a review on the website where you purchased it.

Your review will help other families discover **'My Amazing Preschooler Learning Series'** and help me write more engaging books for young readers.

If you have suggestions or feedback on how to improve this book, please don't hesitate to contact me directly at **zander@tworavensbooks.com.** I greatly value your input!

I'm truly grateful to have you on this learning journey—thank you!

Lee Zander